SONNETS
OF THE
SAVIOUR

CHRISTIAN SHARIFI

Wholesale discounts for book orders are available
through Ingram or Spring Arbor Distributors.

ISBN
978-1-988186-60-3 (softcover)
978-1-988186-58-0 (hardcover)
978-1-988186-59-7 (ebook)

Published in Canada.

First Edition

Dedication

This book is dedicated solely to my Father in heaven, the one that saved my soul and went to the cross for my sins. I give this book in honour of the redemptive work of Jesus Christ on Nazareth, saving humanity from eternal death and leading mankind to life everlasting. He is the Great I Am, Ancient of Days, The Alpha and the Omega and the Creator of all things. He is the one that gives life and also the one that has the power to take it away. My hope for this book is that souls will come to the light of salvation through Jesus Christ and repent to be saved. He has taken me from the brink of death and breathed life to my bones and has blessed me with a new heart that is continually being conformed to his own. I could never imagine a life without God being in complete control of my very being and I marvel daily at the unending love and forgiveness he has shown me. One day true believers of Jesus Christ will be home in their eternal resting place praising the Messiah for everything he has done for us, and what a glorious day that shall be. 2,000 years ago, God himself walked the earth in human form and has payed the price that we deserved for our wickedness. This book belongs to him and my earnest prayer is that he will accept it in his heart of hearts. I dedicate my whole being to God Almighty and am ever so thankful that his Holy Spirit lives within me. I Glorify the name of Jehovah and bless the name of Jesus Christ forever and ever.

CHRISTIAN SHARIFI

SONNETS of the SAVIOUR

Poem 1

In the desert seasons does the man of consecration grow in intimacy

*The duration of his soujournment shall prevail
when the wicked come against thee*

The Lord is seeking those who worship his almighty magnificence

The task master trains his servants for full harvest with labour and diligence

At the right hand of GOD does the childr en of Israel dwell with peace

The horrid stipulations of the unjust shall crumble them at their feet

Exalt the GOD of treaty for he treats his flock with amicable tenderness

*Put the words of the Lord in your prayers and
always have him in remembrance*

A neighbor that acts neighborly to the stranger shall reap treasure unending

The righteous are thrall in their ways and their laws remain unbending

The class of chiefs are classified as royalty amongst a land of heathens

The companion of criminals and thief's remain consistently scheming

The essence of my father is thoughtful, tender and merciful towards the just

The rebellious rascal shall waste his days and will wither and rust

The heart of a lion shall never want or drought in deep hunger

The punishment of the punishers shall strike them as unto thunder

CHRISTIAN SHARIFI

SONNETS OF THE SAVIOUR

Poem 2

Underneath the discipline of the righteous lays laws and measures

Over the flesh of the ungodly engulfs lusts of the body and pleasures

The children of Jehovah are flooded with jewelry and the finest treasures

The offspring of satan shall be plucked off the earth as feathers

The tabernacle of tolerance is jubilation to a lover of GODS word

The refiners' fire dissipates ungodly character as man is purged

Rejoice always in all seasons of life, whether storms or harvests

Woman of GOD shall a bask in meekness and attain to dress modest

A man with the spirit of GOD knows right
from wrong from a living conscious

A corpse dead in their sin, sees wrong as right and is deemed for a coffin

A talebearer tells tales and endures gossip as their past time

A man of prayer and fasting has revelations that seep from the mind

The sound man desires wisdom of his father, and obtains it with no hesitation

A cowardice coward is cowardly and intolerable to the statutes of regulations

The Lord thy GOD is a harbour for my soul and my resting place at ease

He calms the urgency of a matter when the enemy hunts for me

CHRISTIAN SHARIFI

SONNETS of the SAVIOUR

Poem 3

The labourman is worthy of his wages and plays well for the compensation

A false balance is an abomination so pleasure shall stay in moderation

The gain of gold and silver is unto rags compared to the knowledge of Jesus

For by a single offering, all humanity was set free as the Lord redeemed us

The merit of a profitable return shall reap harvest in the day of fury

The surety of a walk of the righteous is a beautiful scent of purity

The foundation of a child must be entrenched with discipline and chastisement

For a man that spares the rod hates his child and does not love him

Never compensate your integrity for false riches of the land

Instead work hard with all your strength and be strong in your hands

Repay the wicked with the wicked side of holiness for defense

The word of GOD must be received with zero contention and offence

A man walking in the mandates of Jehova shall not be tense

Instead divine joy from divine presence shall make immense

In the middle of the congregation, the Holy Spirit takes charge

The enemy and their vial devices shall be cut off and discharged

CHRISTIAN SHARIFI

SONNETS of the SAVIOUR

Poem 4

The death of the unruly is a divine rule and is Holy in nature

For The Lord shall let no unclean thing pass unto his pastures

The Lord shall hear my supplications, as I rise early each morning

The scorns of the scornful are daggers in the heart of the scorning

Let all my enemies be ashamed and sore vexed for their trespasses

My GOD enjoys defending the delicate and punishing foes with set ambushes

He saved me from the persecution and delivered me from pits of Abaddon

His rage rages at the rivals of the righteous as unto a fierce matador

My defender is my GOD and he rescues the upright in heart

He pummels the plans of the perilous and cuts down their fiery darts

Let us celebrate his goodness with an offering of songs and dance

He articulates to me through the means of dreams, visions, and trance

Communication and conversation are the keys to divine guidance

Every second I labour in prayer is gold to my soul and time wise spent

The treacherous shall turn at the turn buckle of a benevolent Creator

The dissolute are devilish in their demeanor and are deemed forbidden traitors

CHRISTIAN SHARIFI

SONNETS OF THE SAVIOUR

Poem 5

A fiery flame of fury frustrates the foes of my fabulous Father

Righteous, pure and moral in his ways, he is a man engulfed with honor

Kindness and meekness are the traits that envelop his faithful character

He blockades the brutal with the Holy Spirit as his offensive barrier

A shepherd to the fatherless, and a father to the orphans of GOD

A heart of obedience, respect and dignity for the statutes of laws

How do I repay the man that his put life into my bones?

What do I give to a King that put vitality into my soul?

Words shall not express the gratitude that encompasses my spirit

He ministers the word of God like fire and my soul desires to hear it

The troubles of the tormenters shall torment them as he prays

With abundance, riches and glory shall my Father live all his days

His heart for his Father is marveled and comparable to king David

He leads his children unto still waters and out of devilish mazes

His understands with understanding the ways of an omnipotent GOD

His defense is angel Michael and angel Gabriel
entrusted with a heavenly squad

CHRISTIAN SHARIFF

SONNETS of the SAVIOUR

Poem 6

Abundant abundance dwells in the chamber of the righteous ones

Poverty of pestilence inhibited the land of the wicked sons

Emasculate joy covers the radiance of the sanctified descendants

By his mercy alone, is man found not guilty as the defendant

Prosperity prospers the children that convey honor

Profoundness personifies the beauty of my Father

Impart into me O LORD, the spirit of thy faith

Grant me the glory my GOD, of the abundance of thy grace

Allow me awe sight, as I enter the house of Elohim

Heal my afflictions, from the enemies' widely schemes

Mt Zion is my nest, the sanctuary of my refuge

Established as a house of prayer and wisdom of thy truths

A thousand days cannot compare to one in your cathedral

Even when the flesh ceases existence, I shall never cease to leave you

Eternal breath lay waiting as I walk thy eternal steps

Infinite blessings pour thunder for I am eternal blessed

CHRISTIAN SHARIFI

SONNETS OF THE SAVIOUR

Poem 7

Evil doers and envious men remain empty as desert landscape

Righteous men walk upright in the heavens where our God's hands have made

Unruly swine who lack honor for the Prince will be destroyed briskly

The enemies of El-Shaddai shall die for he slices them like mincemeat

There is more than one side to the Alpha and the Omega

He is also an avenging warrior at bay that can cause tremendous terror

Yet to His flock, He guards their harvest from the pesky assassins

He travails against the attackers attacks and subdues those savages

He adores the meek of the earth and delights them in abundant peace

My Master is the author of this audacious masterpiece

He is the giver of life, yet the destroyer of the casualty

He destroys the ploys of my foes ensnaring petty traps for me

Mighty defender, mighty avenger, mighty arbor of my days

I adhere to your precepts and run hastefully to obey

The dignity of your grandeur, no man could ever convey

The prestige of your triumph leaves me in constant praise

CHRISTIAN SHARIFI

SONNETS OF THE SAVIOUR

Poem 8

Purify your hearts you sinners, and let the Lord purge your iniquities

For by the fire of the spirit shall he cleanse the unrighteous of their infirmities

The congregation of the sluggard shall reap emptiness on the day of abundance

A dead conscious can do no good while a man
that knows right is alive in conscience

The ruler of the Lords house is the one appointed over the children of GOD

He watches over them and commands fire to
the enemies scattering them abroad

He is plentiful in the word of GOD and adheres to knowledge from the spirit

A cry from a was heard from John in the wilder-
ness and the Lord will surely hear it

Jerusalem is where I shall abode all my days until my Lord arrives in time

Though no man knows the hour, the season, and no man knows the time

The word of GOD are more precious than fine jewels which cease not to shine

His precepts dwell in the duration of my soul
and with my spirit they shall bind

Miraculous miracles followed the Lord as he traveled from city to town

The lion of the tribe of Judah is the king in the
jungle and wears a golden crown

With a meek countenance and a gentle lowly heart he plundered satan's marks

The light of the word illuminates my soul and
gives my spirit an unending spark

CHRISTIAN SHARIFI

SONNETS OF THE SAVIOUR

Poem 9

Open the eyes of my soul and remove a stony heart from my being

Revelation from the Father requires anointed vision and the grace of seeing

The word of the LORD is quicker and sharper than any double edged sword

Two is better than one for their is more strength in the multitudes of cords

A gracious woman retains honor but strong men retain mighty riches

The derision of the tormenter shall give them abundance of painful stiches

Let us not be weary of well doing, for we shall reap if we faint not

As a born again child of GOD, our past sin are no longer an after thought

Above all the King's laws, we must be diligence in fulfilling each one

For in the day of temptation we shall stand mighty as one of the King's sons

Trample the futile attempts of a pitiful enemies endeavors

The Lord shall save the heart of a contrite man and His foes shall He sever

I will sing unto the LORD for He has dealt bountifully with me all my days

Out of the abundance of the heart the mouth speaks so I shall give all my praise

The house of Jacob shall possess all their possessions for it is their inheritance

The tabernacle of Esau shall lose their treasures for the sake of disobedience

CHRISTIAN SHARIFI

SONNETS of the SAVIOUR

Poem 10

Adoration and appreciation of Abel was able and accepted by Abba

Bath of Bethsaida brought benefit and bonus to a bewildered baron

Concise and contrive care of commencing commandments create capital

Discussions about disputes or disagreements drape discord and disturbance

Enchantment of El Shaddai eradicates the evils of evil going exorcists

Flags of the Fathers favor on a farmer are fast finances and funds

A generation that generates generous genes is glorifying to gracious GOD

Habitation of High honor and high standing homage surrounds Hosanna

Irate influx of insidious idolatrous idolaters is idiocy to idiotic idiots

Jump for joyous joy for Jehovah Rapha, Jehovah Nissi, and Jehovah Jah

The King of Khazaria and Kazakhstan are peasants to the King of kingship

Love lavishly and loudly the Lord of Lords across the lands of Lamaria

Meaningful mandates of the majesty bring meaning and maturity

Near Noah's Arch Noah had nasty zeal for nefarious and notorious nomads

Often oscillate omnipotent operas of operation to an omniscient order

Prepare and be poised for poisonous ploys of
pitiful pirates that permeate plunder

CHRISTIAN SHARIFI

SONNETS of the SAVIOUR

Poem 11

My righteous rock is solid and can never be dismantled by diabolical devils

I look past the firmament of the skies and seek promotion to another level

Diverse temptations have zero effect on a man rich in the word of truth

For His foundations is a fortress of armory and He is strengthened at the roots

He castrates wicked whore mongers in a grave of grieven images

He handcrafted the world and the heavens in the midst of perfect symmetry

Howbeit that a fool can believe in his wicked heart that there is no GOD

While a man of laws and rules rejoices in the beauty of His adoring Awe

Blessing and honor pours down like rain and snow on the head of the sanctified

While thieves and criminals attain no morality and cease not to act defiled

Your Kingdom shall reign over all the Earth and the unrepentant shall perish

Every tongue on Heaven and Earth rejoice in our
GOD for your splendor we cherish

From Nazareth to the deepest depths of Damascus,
man is a corpse without GOD

For in His righteousness we are made perfect though no man is empty of flaws

His faithful love endures past the begin-
nings and ends of time that He assembled

The heathens thoughts are ancient in their endeavors and shall remain simple

CHRISTIAN SHARIFI

SONNETS of the SAVIOUR

Poem 12

An influx of hazards are the roadway for the judged of the judge

The meek in spirit are privy to forgive while the evil hold grudge

The groans of the grievous are a delight to Jehovah and his statutes

Obedience of the Word of God is choice in which one must grasp to

Too many slanderers and extortioners roam the streets at night

Jehovah will blind their eyes to cinder and disassemble their sight

The path of a labourer produces fine crops in the middle of a drought

The boulevard of a laggard shall yield sorrow and mournful shouts

Coals of indignation burn the indignitaries of injustice

Embers of enchantment devour the streams of the righteous

Slander and deceit are the rivers of water in a ravenous beast

The king's delicacies are prepared at the wedding supper feast

A prophet is the head of a congregation and is frank in his manner

A man that serves his own flesh is a man prone to vengeful anger

Humiliation harbours at the harbour of the sorcerers and witches

Warlocks and jezebels shall lay in waste places and eternal ditches

CHRISTIAN SHARIFI

SONNETS OF THE SAVIOUR

Poem 13

The trials and tribulations of the of the tormented torments them

The manner of the mild and meek makes them a majestic majesty

The yearning of the yielding yokes them with Yahweh

The bravery is the brave is born of benevolence and boldness

The adulterers are atrocious and act as animals always

The silence of the simple simplifies sour situations

The lowly linger in liability and live in lasting luxury

Wicked whoremongers wreak and waste weeks upon weeks in whoredom

The glorified gaze at the gorgeousness of a giant God

The stipulations of the sodomites stay from summer to spring

The nefarious nomads norm is notorious as a Neanderthal

The veraciousness of the vagabonds vexes their vitality

Dormant dunes of despair drought the dukes of desolation

The planks of a pirate are the paths of pestilence for the poisonous

Gates of glory are garnished for the galloping in God

CHRISTIAN SHARIFI

SONNETS OF THE SAVIOUR

Poem 14

The defiled are diseased with drought and dyer death

The Holy hang handsomely in the hands of Hosanna

The veritable are very vigorous and vital with vitality

Woe waits for the whores who want to worship the world

Do not depart from the door to Damascus

Born out of betrayal was Babylon and it's brutes

Stay steadfast storming swiftly to the sands of Samaria

In Lebanon lies lofty luxuries for the lenient and the lowly

In Bethlehem born by beauty but bewildered by brazen bastards

Herod was hideous, horrible and hazardous to Hosannas heart

Arrest the angry and agonize their ancestry

Generation genes generate galled genealogy

Follow fastly not falsely to forever's family

Righteously and rigorously read the rulers rules

Mans motives must model the mandate of Messiah

Jolt with jubilation and joy and join journeys with Jesus

SONNETS of the SAVIOUR

Poem 15

The gracious sons of men adore his brilliant enigma

The separation between man and God was the definition of dilemma

In a world of deceit, chaos and confusion

Only through Elohim may man see past the allusions

Jehovah is a fortress that can never be demolished

The righteous labor in the field, so patient for the harvest

Jesus is a name that shall never have tarnish

The Creator of all things, we celebrate the artist

My Majesty is a marvel, His word reads as a novel

The fate of the faithless ends in a manner worse than awful

In prayer and supplication I come humbly before the King

In songs of adulation, with excellence I shall sing

The firmament is a wonder, his power is as thunder

If I die for Jesus Christ, the world knows me as martyr

If the rapture comes this eve, then home I am abound

I enter the throne room of my God, with pride I wear my crown

CHRISTIAN SHARIFI

SONNETS of the SAVIOUR

Poem 16

The sexually sinful and the sorcerers solicit in Sodom

Gomorrah is grotesque in the gravity of it gross-ness

Inhabitants of Israel isolate themselves from infirmities and idolatry

The faith of the faithful fuels their fire forever

The doubtful drown in diverse derision and debauchery

The river of redemption runs rightfully in the righteous

The ocean of overwhelming overcomes the obscene and offensive

The Peace of the peaceful polishes the pure as porcelain

The lying liars lie in lakes of locusts and lizards

The obedience of the obedient oscillates as an orb

The sultry of the source of salvation shines like the savior

The gruesome gasp for gluttonous and grody goods

The wisdom of the wise wires their ways into wealth

The heathens hellish hunger for hideousness hands them to hell

The angels awe at the amazing adoration of Abba

The bona fide bask in the beauty and brilliance of his boldness

The wicked are worms in a worm pool of wrathful wrath

The Lord love landed in my lap in luminosities and light

CHRISTIAN SHARIFI

SONNETS OF THE SAVIOUR

Poem 17

The transgressors path of life is the path of death

The righteous road to redemption leads to the palace steps

Envy strife and malice are the same as an anvil around thy neck

Faith, love and grace are the life that gives us breath

The power to forgive comes from the power high above

The virtue to love thy neighbor will soar you like a dove

The generous shall remain as pillars on the earth

While the greedy suffer agony and abundance of the hurt

The wicked shall flee when no man pursueth them

The righteous are bold as a lion for there is much truth in them

The vultures are volatile and vain in their veins

The sanctified love chastisement and have the ability to change

The Holy give homage to the Holy one in heaven

The venomous speak guile and wait for their poison just to set in

The asunder of the absurd shall cause havoc to the heathen

While the glory of the glorious glorify our lives with meaning

CHRISTIAN SHARIFI

SONNETS OF THE SAVIOUR

Poem 18

Jehovah's tyranny causes terror to the treacherous/

Yet his kindness kindles the cares of the heaven scent

The righteous are a bold as a lion feasting it's prey

The matador manifests on the wicked and leaves them astray

Messiahs monarchy marches forward until his time

No man knows the hour, when he arrives in our skies

If the tribe of Issachar held the grace to know the seasons

Then man must meditate the word to be set free from the price of treason

As he rest upon the cross, his body was yet bleeding

Without him my life is vain, without God I have no meaning

The sacrifice of his son was summoned to save our souls

The glory of my God gleams greater than the gold

Heaven hails Halleluja, while angels revel in bliss

Judas was the traitor who betrayed him with a kiss

The wisdom of Paul was appaling, even Peter proclaimed it un parallel

To his deciples he confounded all truths, to the crowd he spoke in parables

CHRISTIAN SHARIFI

SONNETS OF THE SAVIOUR

Poem 19

The journey to Judeah and Jerusalem made Jesus the jewel of Jehovah

The monarchy of the Messiah is mandated for magnificence

Behold the bravery and the beauty of the born begotten

Glorify the glorious grandeur of my Gods greatest gift

Astonished by his amazing affection and adulation

The fire and the flame fuming in my furnace is forever

The tyrant terrorizes the treacherous and torments them

He kindles the kindhearted kindly with a kiss

He subdues the schemes and the snares of the sinful

The ploys and plots of the perilous are painful

The rage roaring the repulsive renders them reprobate

The evil endure until epilepsy envelops them

Jehovah is justly in his judgements and jurisdiction

For Jehovah is the judge, the jury, and the justice for the jail bound

Howbeit he holds the Holy half-pints in his hands

Eternally enveloping my emperor with enchantment

CHRISTIAN SHARIFI

SONNETS of the SAVIOUR

Poem 20

The destroyer destroyed the depraved dungeons of the deprived

The royalty radiant in regal ruling renownment

The fairness of the Father facilitates friendship from his fondness

Saturated by his sovereignty saturating spirit and soul

Fouls of fatherless fornicators form fatal fires for the flagrant

Could calamity corrupt the corruptible choices of the carnal

The whisper of a whispering widow will worship his wonderful wonders

The sediments of the Savior is saluted by societies saved souls

The sacrifice was sufficient for the surplus of suffering for Saviors saints

Long lasting long suffering and lingering laceration lamented the lowly

Everlasting envelopment of endearment endeared the elders

Escape from the exercises and exorcists of evil empty enchanters

Flee from factious fools that formulate in flamboyant fairytales

A desperate desire to dwell in the dwelling of dignity is desirable

Adversary, ache, afflictions, and agony assimilate ample abundance

Insane idolatry of impure idiots is inferior to impartial innocence

CHRISTIAN SHARIF

SONNETS of the SAVIOUR

Poem 21

The world spins on an access of beauty made perfect

My God gives worth to the ones who felt previously worthless

He heals the wounds of the saints who suffered affliction

He mends their hearts from the agony of the incision

He restores wasteplaces and empty landfills to prosperity

He amends insane minds to the point of mental clarity

He brings fourth riches and power to humble in heart

He protects us from the ravenous wolves and wicked sharks

His plan is to enrich us with a rich life of joy

He is poised to deploy warfare angels to battle and destroy

He came as the lamb of God but is enthroned as the lion

He sits at his throne with royalty and as a giant of giants

He radiates light and peace across the heavens abroad

In the beginning was the word and the word was with God

He answers the prayers of the people walking in integrity

Let us all bless the name of The Lord from now until infinite

CHRISTIAN SHARIFI

SONNETS OF THE SAVIOUR

Poem 22

I praise my God in the mornings before dawn awakes

I praise my God forevermore for that is the essence of faith

I praise my God in the sanctuary with the brethren

I praise my God across the earth and the heavens

I praise my God because he gave me breath to breathe

I praise my God because he blesses me with all my needs

I praise my God because he always puts manna on my plate

I praise my God for his greatness is everlastingly great

I praise my God because His words give life to my bones

I praise my God because he sent his son to save my soul

I praise my God for it brings me peace that surpasses understanding

I praise my God even if I am the lone man standing

CHRISTIAN SHARIFI

SONNETS OF THE SAVIOUR

Poem 23

My shepherd protects me from dangers and vile snares of evil

My shepherd is a fortress of armor and defense for his people

My shepherd is the greatest of the great, to him there is no equal

My shepherd is loyal to his chosen sons, he shall never leave you

My shepherd saved the lives of millions because of his great sacrifice

My shepherd put me on the golden road to heaven in the afterlife

My shepherd has my heart my soul and all my trust in his hands

My shepherd is a tower of might and wonder and his kingdom shall stand

My shepherd is the light on my path in my darkest hours

My shepherd is a fire on the camps of the ones who seek to devour

My shepherd is kind, merciful and gracious to the ones he endures

My shepherd gives abundance to the Holy and the ones who are pure

My shepherd gives me grace to pursue him with all my passion

My shepherd hears my prayers every single time I ask him

My shepherd will soon take away his children to the city above

My shepherd is named the Prince of Peace and soars as a dove

CHRISTIAN SHARIFI

SONNETS of the SAVIOUR

Poem 24

The favor of the Father is forever finalized on my footpath

Messiahs mercy is magnificent for the monarchs of majesty

Creator Christ came to corrode the corruptible and calamitous

Destruction and disaster is deemed for the defiled demons of death

Prospering in prosperity is proclaimed for pure people of purity

What a wonderful wonder waits for wholesome woman with wings

The tyranny of a tyrant terminates the terminated thieves

Excitement and enchantment enthrall enrolment in Eden

Diverse derision defecates devilish and dangerous deities

Calamity collides the caskets of cons and contentious citizens

Vexation vapours the vagabonds in vast valleys of volcanoes

Vibrant vibrancy is the vibration for valour and virtuousness

Seek the sacred sediments sustaining soul and spirit in synchronism

God's grace is given to the gracious and generous genes

Angry armies of Abba attack atrocious alliances at Armageddon

Wrongs of the wicked and wrathful wastes them in a whirlpool of woes

CHRISTIAN SHARIFI

SONNETS of the SAVIOUR

Poem 25

Plead my strife O' Lord, with those that fight for my death
Draw out thy spear and thy sword and slay my enemies around
Show no mercy upon my rivals, ending with corpses left
Let the battle ground be the burial ground as my enemies fret

He that deviseth mischief, is a drought without the rain
He that upholds thy laws, is a soul basking in serenity
He that exhorts your Word, is a man beyond the pain
He that gives to the poor, is a man who's fit to gain

To give is to live, while to withhold is to grow old
Give to the poor, give to the widows, and give to your beloved brethren
Giving shall always fall back in your harvest and give life unto your soul
He gave his only begotten son, now we walk the heavenly roads

The Lord knows the days of the upright, and their inheritance is forever
He blesses the blessings of the angelic, and gives them gold in their baskets
He cuts down the life of the unjust, as if their days was always never
He holds his own in his nets, but to the wicked ones he severs

CHRISTIAN SHARIFI

SONNETS OF THE SAVIOUR

Poem 26

Jesus Christ is the image of perfection to an ungodly and dying generation

Victorious as the great victor , he is a marvel of undying celebration.

The pursuit of joy is beyond the elements of natural life

For joy is a supernatural cause, which comes down from the Father of lights

A daily dose of the word of God shall quicken a man's spirit

When God speaks , the spirit of revelation shall empower a man to see it

The lame shall walk, the blind shall see, and the deaf shall hear

The wicked flee when no man pursueth for they are in a constant state of fear

The laws of liberty I shall meditate in all my days adhere

The sorrows of the sorrowful are mournful always shedding tears

Let the nations of the earth, give glory to the God of glorification

Let the kings offer sacrifices of dance for their God is a God of fortification

For what cause does a unrepentant sinner have any right to breathe

Their unruly hearts device torments by all and any means

The rulers of railers and traitors shall fall in a pit of lava

They shall suffer vexation with boils of boiling water

CHRISTIAN SHARIFI

SONNETS of the SAVIOUR

Poem 27

The kings' favor is towards the Godly, but shame soaks the amoral

The righteous live in peaceful bliss, while the sinner basks in constant quarrel

The atrocious antagonist is deviated in his ways and has a heart of stone

The froward lips of a thief shall make his days filled with painful groans

The Lord condones kindness and care to the careful and meek in spirit

He separates the sinners from the saints and the wicked are always fearing

Every way of man is right in his own eyes but the Lord ponders their hearts

The diligent deacon of obedience shall reign on earth and make a mighty mark

Justice and judgement embodies modest and pabulum peers of purity

A man who is redeemed by the blood of Jesus lives in absolute surety

Serene servants of submission are unassuming and yielding in the fields

My Lord delivers and protects my marrow and guards me as a shield

Immodest idols of idolatry is in daily derision as the Lord evokes anger

Be careful to entangle relations with the lips of a woman who is a stranger

The Lord shall exalt the humble while the self-exalted shall he humble

He is the light upon my feet, yet the unyield-
ing shall he cause cancer and crumble

CHRISTIAN SHARIFI

SONNETS OF THE SAVIOUR

Poem 28

The enemy's nefarious snares are without cause or justice

While the light of salvation protects me like the summer solstice

I hunger for thy word, no more do I desire any ration

Ignited inside by a ferocious unquenchable passion

The Lord in his Holy temple, watches over the wise

In His sanctuary He stands, placing judgement upon their crimes

In the synagogue of valor, His majesty reigns supreme

Unveiling through revelation, the truths that are unseen

The words of the Lord are pure words as of gold

The speech of the Savior, shall make my foes just fold

How many days have passed, since I've seen you face to face

The wasted me has vanished, with no sign or no trace

His commandments are not grievous, so I treasure them inside

His laws inhibit my marrow, and save me from the trials

His precepts gain me favor , with both man and my GOD

His dictates dictate peace, in a world deceived by fraud

CHRISTIAN SHARIFI

SONNETS of the SAVIOUR

Poem 29

Jehovah is my shield, on the frontlines of war
Elohim is my protector, my Father, and my Lord
Emanuel is so Holy, God is always with us
Jesus Christ lives within me, my love and my trust

The Holy Spirit is power, the Holy Spirit is strength
Jehovah grants blessings, my GOD grants me wealth
His armory is my armor, his hands are like potters
Creating the beauty of the worlds, his presence I long for

He's a prince that reigns peace in our hearts
His power delivered my groans from the midst of the dark
He is a protector of evil, shielding me from the sharks
He destroys the wickedness of the wicked, before they even start

Praise to the highest God, a gasp in his beauty
Glory to the King of Glory, He destroys the unruly
Hallelujah to the Messiah, worship Him with Holy songs
He forgave us for our sins, He showed mercy for our wrongs

CHRISTIAN SHARIFI

SONNETS of the SAVIOUR

Poem 30

In the midst of persecution I shall never fall on my knees

For my inheritance in Christ has thou prepared for me

In the midst of tribulation I shall magnify you indeed

For the word tells us to be doers of the word in action and in deeds

In the midst of agony I shall sing songs from the tabernacle of my soul

Mt. Zion is my restoration ground, on an open road I go

In the midst of tormentors, I follow my God in His stature

Early will I seek thee for I believe to receive the answer

In the midst of my enemies, I sacrifice with burnt offerings

Abraham has trained me to rejoice even in my sufferings

In the midst of unyielding disputes, I adore His word each day

I am merely just a man but through His power I receive grace

In the midst of endless worriment, I shall still pray for my brethren

As I come before the throne of grace, my fellows I shall mention

In the midst of distress and derision I find way to praise and worship

*Out of my belly shall flow rivers of flowing water
for my God created my purpose*

CHRISTIAN SHARIFI

SONNETS of the SAVIOUR

Poem 31

My Lord thy God, avenge your son from the hands of poisonous pythons

In Christ I am a new creation thus my sins are merely bygones

My Lord thy God, protect me from the snare of envious Extortioners

In a world of sorcerers , drunkards , and vile abortioners

My Lord thy God, why do ungodly men even have the right to breathe

For by vain imaginations they run from enemies they cannot see

My Lord thy God, I am at wits end over sodomites that come near my path

Cut them down at the root and set a blaze upon their beaten paths

My Lord thy God, your wings give me peace In the day of trouble

Break down Goliath's army , and turn his counterparts to rubble

My Lord thy God, in your presence I find peace and prosperity

Let your mind be in mine so I can envision visions of clarity

My Lord thy God, in the day of affliction your buckler is my safe belt

Burn my adversaries alive and vex them sore as their flesh melts

My Lord thy God, as I pray in the spirit your power is highly magnified

Your righteousness exalted a nation , by your blood I am sanctified

Poem 32

His ordinances have ordained me for a hefty exaltation

His precepts I shall ensue, until the epoch of His celebration

Prior to dawn, I moxie before Jehovah at His glorious throne of grace

I spiel to him my desires eternal, through the means of supplication

I deprive myself of ration, for the heart of His affection

I speak the word of God in trials, knowing it's the light of protection

The joy of Jehovah is a joy beyond space and time

I seek him earnestly, exalting this mighty grace of mine

I am the apple of His eye, the shadow beneath His wings

I delight in His winter, I gasp in His springs

The Lord is my rock, my fortress, and my castle

The Lord is my shield, my barrier, and my mantle

My God knows all my attractions, and the ways of my ardor

Born again in the spirit, one could assert I am a martyr

He sends His arrows on the sparrows plotting my death

He mocks my mockers with mockery, until there soul gasps for one last breath

SONNETS of the SAVIOUR

Poem 33

The pillars of Mt. Zion stand firm like the oak wood in the forest

The rage of the antagonist shall leave the unruly constrained and sore vexed

The world is a paradox, with such beauty yet malice deceit

Be not thou envious of the oppressor, for their souls are diseased

Convey love, honesty, and virtue in the bonds of your affairs

The one that created the earth and its suns shall not let you despair

Howbeit that the wicked speak guile, and shall not go unpunished

When your enemies angle antagonism, thou shalt only love them

How many grains of sand, rest on the beaches of the shore?

How many thoughts does our God ponder on our souls?

How many snowflakes touchdown on a winters evening?

Though tribulations thou has overcome that givest life thy meaning

The God of constellations give me thou consolation

We regard the works of your hands, and the art of your operations

The righteous shall flourish, while the wicked are in constant wailing

I shall be a man of worship, a man of constant praising

CHRISTIAN SHARIFI

SONNETS of the SAVIOUR

Poem 34

For basic Instructions before I leave Earth I shall look to the bible

The word of GOD out of my mouth is unto a loaded rifle

Manifest His manifestations by vocalizing His vocab

To not dwell with the Holy Spirit is to remain a lonely nomad

The power to perform is sworn into the vessel of man

By His word did he conceive the universe before the world began

The conception of mankind, was born by Adam and Eve

The serpent deceived them with trickery, and hoaxed them with his schemes

The Garden was their castle, perfected by its perfection

A wonderland of paradise, a safe haven of protection

But sin was the cause of their hateful revocation

They left the land of blossom, unto the flower of a lotus

A life destitute of the Father, shall leave thy spirit always mundane

While the joyful rejoice evermore, and the evil shall complain

In the tabernacle of Jehovah, shall the blameless rise in splendor

By thanksgiving and by praise, I have a means to enter

CHRISTIAN SHARIFI

SONNETS of the SAVIOUR

Poem 35

The people of God are peculiar in the way they live their lives

An ocean of vastness differentiates the chil-
dren of the devil and the children of Christ

Some live after the flesh and the lusts thereof,
while the saints breathe in the spirit

The only thing to fear is fear itself, so in death there is no reason to fear it

Many live as mundane monsters, while the off-
spring of GOD remain firmly planted

Through obedience the obedient are blessed as they
follow Jehovah's commandments

If hell truly exists, then so does heaven, so where will you spend eternity?

You either carry the spirit of the father, or house the spirit of infirmities

Days have gone by, years have passed as the
wind, yet few have found salvation

As I glorify the King of Glory, often times I witness evil and mad faces

Why do the heathen rage? When their snares are futile as fungus

Why do the righteous blossom? Because their pro-
tector defends them from troubles

The world is a mirror of counterfeit created to deceive the masses in slavery

While the kingdom of God shall leave a taste in our hearts worth savoring

The life of a born again, shall lead them into a path that is sworn to win

While the life of the unrepentant soul shall leave them cleaved and sworn to sin

CHRISTIAN SHARIFI

SONNETS of the SAVIOUR

Poem 36

Ravenous ravens roam in Rome raging rivalry right at the royalty of royalties

Pursuing the Prince of Peace is a ploy of poison to pernicious pirates

Death, destruction, dismay, and debauchery is the diary of the defiled

Havoc of hell to the heinous, harmful, and hideous heathens has hit home

Gruesome Goliath the giant gazed at the generals of GOD and got guillotined

Heartless Harod had a horrific heart attack
having hideous honor for Hosanna

Pharaoh plotted and ployed perilously putting the people of purity in prison

Pessimistic pharisees planned perilousness to the prime power at Passover

Jehovah was just in His judgement jolted at the jurors of Jerusalem

The surplus of sin saddened the Savior yet He saved a spiteful society

Fabrications of the froward and fornicators were forged at the Father

Tribulation, torment, and trials of torture and trouble travailed to the titans

God gave the grievous and gruesome ghouls a goliath gob of grief and gloom

Bewildered by baron buffoons but bestowed
burdens on the betrayals of the betrayer

Salute the Savior and stay in servanthood to slay the shackles of sodomites

Magnify the magnificent majestic marvelous marvel of my Master's master

CHRISTIAN SHARIFI

SONNETS of the SAVIOUR

Poem 37

How many stars flood the skies beauty as we gaze at the image of brilliance

The number is an endless number surpassing the infinite by the millions

How many grains of sand sit at the shores of oceans overwhelmed by artistry

Only the omniscient one is portrayed by the beauty of His salutary

The vitality of the world lays at the handwork of the one who designed it

No words of mankind could ever truly por-
trays the glory of our Fathers enticement

Man must seek with all his strength and heart to enter into the heart of God

While much of humanity consumes the lusts of
the flesh and this wicked worlds facet

My God and my Father's ways, shall always
remain the same for He changes not

The rebelliousness of mankind provokes him to
anger and daily makes him wroth

He is wonderful to the humble at heart, but is a judge to the prideful soul

The treasure of the believer is His spirit, as if man was mining gold

Yet diamonds, gems, and rubies, shall never amount to the glory my father

He destroys as the destroyer, to the rebels who show him lack of honor

Victory is saturated in the throne room of my mighty GOD Jehovah

Without His spirit I will fall, but with His spirit
abiding I am man made to soldier

CHRISTIAN SHARIFI

SONNETS of the SAVIOUR

Poem 38

The Creator created with creativity creation

With wisdom and understanding did he construct the amazing

Heaven is a haven which no man can perceive

His beauty is beautified and gives me life to breathe

His kingdom is a portrayal of perfection imagined

The pleasure of royalty living lives beyond lavish

The cross created credence for eternal salvation

Let all the saints give glory to my Fathers Holy nation

His mercy entrenched man from generation to generation

Destroying the barrier of communication and separation

The mind cannot fathom His glory with imagination

By the blood of Jesus Christ I have besought eternal transformation

A wonder to mankind, and a wonder to His angels

Born in Bethlehem, in the midst of a manger

The wise men brought gifts for their God when he was born

He took away the strife, and he washed away my scorns

CHRISTIAN SHARIFI

SONNETS OF THE SAVIOUR

Poem 39

His everlasting joy shall be the brightness of my countenance

He is my strength, my shield, my sword, and my confidence

His mercy endureth past the outer reaches of the plains

The world shall rejoice in the mighty calling of his name

The birds of the air, and the beast of the field shall know their maker

So creative as he created the worlds is our wonderful Creator

The inhabitants of His throne dwell in abundant peace

Give to the Lord a bountiful offering to show he is amongst thee

How long shall the wicked plan their guile and deceit

A day shall come, when the Lord entangles their feet

He is a God of judgement, a God that reigns ambushments

But the righteous beget mercy, the wicked shall not push them

Praise be to the most high God, the mighty King of Israel

He shall burn the flesh on the flaming throne of the infidel

Execute your judgements, on the liars and the scorners

And have no pity, as their cohorts try to mourn them

CHRISTIAN SHARIFI

SONNETS OF THE SAVIOUR

Poem 40

The chief and the commander command closing curtains for the callous

A skilled servant is skillful as a soldier with a savory soul of the Savior

The masterful master the meaningful mandates of the majestic mogul

The reigning ruler rules with rules and restrictions for the rightward

The conductor conducts controlling control like Caesar in the city

A direct dignitary is a director of direc-
tion to the diverse dwellers of Damascus

Political people provide pure policies proclaiming prescribed precepts

Regulations regulate rags and redeem the righteousness of the righteous

The charges in the charter are codes of conduct and caveats to the community

A decisive decision demanded by the deity decreed derision on the damnable

Disasters and destruction are the demotion of the depraved dwellers

Humankind has to horde humanitarianism and honor to other humans

The fatherless are fixated with the flesh and are fallible with fallacies

Beastly beasts are brutishly brute and body beastliness and are baneful

Intense inspiration influence the intention of impulsive icons

My master's master is a master of motivation and his motives are marvelous

CHRISTIAN SHARIFI

SONNETS OF THE SAVIOUR

Poem 41

Journey with me, to the beauty of the promise land

The wicked shall not enter, but heaven rejoices the honest man

From Genesis to Revelation, his words breathe life

From the beginning to the end, my heart endureth Christ

Why should man perish? When eternal life awaits us

Repent of your sins, and thou cast away your lusts

When he created the heavens, we were still in his thoughts

For mankind to be safeguarded, it flared with a cost

It is the price of his blood, that a las we are secured

Persecution and treachery, our Savior did endure

His nature is so gentle, his character is so pure

Sin was our avocation, his blood was the only cure

He actualized eternity, with the ploy of his fingers

The joy of the Lord, is my countenance for it lingers

Cease not to dance for the majestic Son of GOD

Forever shall I sing, for Jesus redeemed us all

SONNETS of the SAVIOUR

Poem 42

The rain which falls from the heavens is akin to the abundance for the meek

Develop intimacy as we enter the throne of grace and my God shall I seek

The emperor halts for the chosen few to come before His throne room with joy

The enemy believes they are coy but there pitiful ploys shall be destroyed

The shield of the sun shields His sons from deception and dyer agony

The death of the wicked is deemed righteous but the
death of the righteous is deemed tragedy

The mountain of my GOD is a climb not ordained for the faint of heart

The cross on cavalry was ordained for souls of GOD to escape the dark

From city to city, the countries give homage to the benevolent general

His handwork of creation remains a wonder and the definition of a spectacle

From the smallest of particles of sand, to the most minute minerals

Jehova my God created from the spirit and it manifested into the physical

If the storm of life is a beacon of destruction then Jehovah is my absorber

The wisdom of God is revealed by the spirit of truth who constantly informs us

The bulwark of armament is a buffer against the ones who cause bafflement

Eden was the presence of God, and in that Garden man shall find contentment

CHRISTIAN SHARIFI

SONNETS OF THE SAVIOUR

Poem 43

The infinite spirit of the infinite one reigns until infinite

The journey of the righteous lay at the hands of the GOD of destiny

The flight to favor sojourns at the land of wisdom and knowledge

He gave breath in my lungs, and soul to my spirit, my Creator I acknowledge

Let the dead bury the dead, but let the living in Christ rejoice forever

For their sins have been redeemed at the cross as if they were never

The prodigal son walked in prodigality and left His Father's order

He roamed the streets in shame and torment from border upon border

Until the day finally came, where he truly repented in his heart

And the Father was rejoiced that His son was rescued from all the sharks

In the same manner, does our Father in heaven rejoice when man submits

All the transgressions of the past, does my God through mercy forget

No man was ever righteous, no not even one

God himself came as a man, and bore a generation of sons

The cross was the greatest day of glory in the history of mankind

The Lord Jesus Christ bore our sins and wiped the misery from man's mind

CHRISTIAN SHARIFI

SONNETS OF THE SAVIOUR

Poem 44

He reigns from the pillars of his majestic kingdom

Obedience attainted from willingness to listen

The Father sent the Son, ordained on a mission

The purpose was to redeem, fulfilling the vision

Through our King, we liberate from being perished

Through our High Priest, his sacrifice is to cherish

My heart yearns for his spirit to relish

He was willing to recompense the ransom

Now we have eternal life, beside our heavenly mansions

A flame has been ignited inflamed with passion

Let us stand in awe, at his unending adulation

Giving us the saints, the ministry of reconciliation

The eponym of Jehovah, is one that lives enduringly

His kindness and mercy is one that forever nurtures me

My voice shall thou hear, in the mornings at last

My cries He hearkens evermore, my soul is grasped

CHRISTIAN SHARIFI

SONNETS OF THE SAVIOUR

Poem 45

The commandments of God shall command bless-
ings on the man that shall oblige

The judgement of God shall severe the heads of the sinners that desire to die

The harvest of the honorable separates them from the snares of evil men

I beseech you brethren that while you live on
earth that you steadfast flee from sin

Do not desire riches over God, for death is doomed for haughty businessmen

The verdict of the victorious one shall be handed once and not again

Be wise, and choose the virtuous path that the Almighty has ordained for you

The world is full of lies and deceit, yet the Word
of God shall always remain the truth

Write the words of the Lord on the deep tablets of your heart and follow them

The multitudes are baron of the word in their soul so they waste as hollow men

Nation after nation esteems El Shaddai for His glamour and greatness

The world is a mere matrix created by the devil so do not believe the fakeness

The people of the lands praise the prestige the high standing of Jehovah

The one that created the heavens and the earth created you, O' how he knows us

Man's thoughts and desires have become depraved of dignity and valor

Most men's faith has been shipwrecked by an enormous ominous anchor

CHRISTIAN SHARIFI

SONNETS OF THE SAVIOUR

Poem 46

The tabernacle of traitors and thieves is a tall tornadoes of torture

Flagrant and froward fellows flee far from the fortunate and their fortune

Diabolical devils deliberate death blows to deceived and desecrated deacons

Radically and radiant royals revere the rise of regnant and renowned rulers

Roaring rage of the regal is righteous reserved for risky and riotous rats

Feeble folks and their first families are frustrated
from forfeiture of the Father's fathoms

All of Abbas archangels assist in the awe and amaz-
ingly astonishment of the Almighty

Under the undertow of unhuman, uncivil and uncivi-
lized underclass is the undertaker

The code of charters of the Creator's constitutions correlate cosmic creation

Dangerous disarming and debilitating decrees distinguish death like dynamite

Mortal men marvel at the magnified majes-
ties of the monarch of marvelousness

For the Father's favorite we forever feel favor even in frustrating facets

Born in the best and brilliantly beautiful beaches we boldly bless our begetter

I beseech you brethren be gone with bygones and let bygones be bygone

Formulas to fix frustrated foul and forbid footings fit with our Father's father

Why wait to wonder about the wonders of the wondrous and wonderful world

CHRISTIAN SHARIFI

SONNETS of the SAVIOUR

Poem 47

The mountain of God is a refuge for the redeemed in Christ

They were once blinded in their eyes, but behold, now they see the light

Inside them burns the vengeance of a soldier ordained to fight

Fulfilling the law of full obedience to the Father's delight

They trivial against the pitiful schemes of the scornful

They adhere to the Creator's ways and make the ravenous mournful

Intelligence of the mind is a gift from God alone

Spiritual impartation is a treasure from my Gods throne

A palace of paradise is awaits for the sons of man in Eden

A land of torment torments the tormenters who were always heathens

The Father's love is eternal and unconditional to His children

Their pieces were once broken as pots, but His desire was to fix them

When the Father created the earth, the wind, and the stars

Is the same time when he created Pluto, Jupiter, and Mars

The radiance of the ruler reigns past Armageddon

The resilience of His power goes past His arms extension

CHRISTIAN SHARIFI

SONNETS of the SAVIOUR

Poem 48

The mind, the body, the soul and the spirit are all one

Jehovah my God's glory shines brighter than an infinite of suns

Who could ever attempt to dethrone the king's throne without dismay

The resurrection of the Lord Jesus Christ was forever the greatest day

All of the sins of humanity, were burned at the foot of the cross

The devil and his cohorts feel the agony of a defiant loss

The trust in my bones is deep like the valleys in the ocean

He restored all my waste places, giving life to all my emotions

The Father manifests His glory based on perfect timing

The word of God is gold, be a miner that is in constant mining

The fire and the hammer, shall break the rock into pieces

The rock of my salvation, is given to mighty Jesus

Relentless in His missions that the Father sent him fourth

The sinners shall be judged in the place of heavenly courts

The course that gives me credence, has landed in His hands

The defender of the brethren, has defected evil plans

CHRISTIAN SHARIFI

SONNETS of the SAVIOUR

Poem 49

Rebellious rebels raise rigorous riots against royalties' royals

Jehovah's just and justified justly jump for joy in joyous jolly

Persistent peace portrays the pleasantly pleased people of the palace

Dementia deathly dagger derives the diluted demons of dormancy

The saturation of the sun sparkles the saved soldiers of the Savior's son

The infiniteness of immortality is illustrated at the initiation of imagination

Lustful loathsome liars lay lonely like Lazarus in lamentations and laceration

Irritable and irate idols are infiltrated by idola-
try and are inflamed in ill-temper

Often offensive and outraged orphans are obscene and overly overt

Allurement and attractions are always the anchor of angelic angels

Immensely Intense illness, injury and irritation infects the intolerable

Vindictive and venomous vultures are vermin and vial in vexations

Perplex paradox of parallels portray for people of purity to people of poison

Repulsiveness repels ravishingly from repugnant and rebellious revolters

Calamity castrates the chiefs of Caesar for continu-
ous corruption and criminal conduct

The main mischief of misery and misfortune is man in His malignity

CHRISTIAN SHARIFI

SONNETS of the SAVIOUR

Poem 50

The shadow of Peter had the power to heal the multitudes

The Lord shall exalt the lowly who seek to walk in servitude

Paul the chief apostle had wisdom beyond his peers

For his understanding came from GOD so it was wisdom beyond years

James had revelations forgoing a man's journey unto faith

For a man to reach his designed destiny, he must reign in grace

In prayer we manifest our most earnest desires

We can command blessings and healings and also release fire

The love of God is not without the agony of his wrath

The peace of God is the greatest gift one can have

Temptation comes in many different shapes and forms

The spirit of the living God has the power to transform

When the enemies' snares come at you like a swarm

The spirit of my Father will always speak to warn

Sinners lives are trampled and their hearts are merely torn

The day I accept my Jesus, was the day that I was born

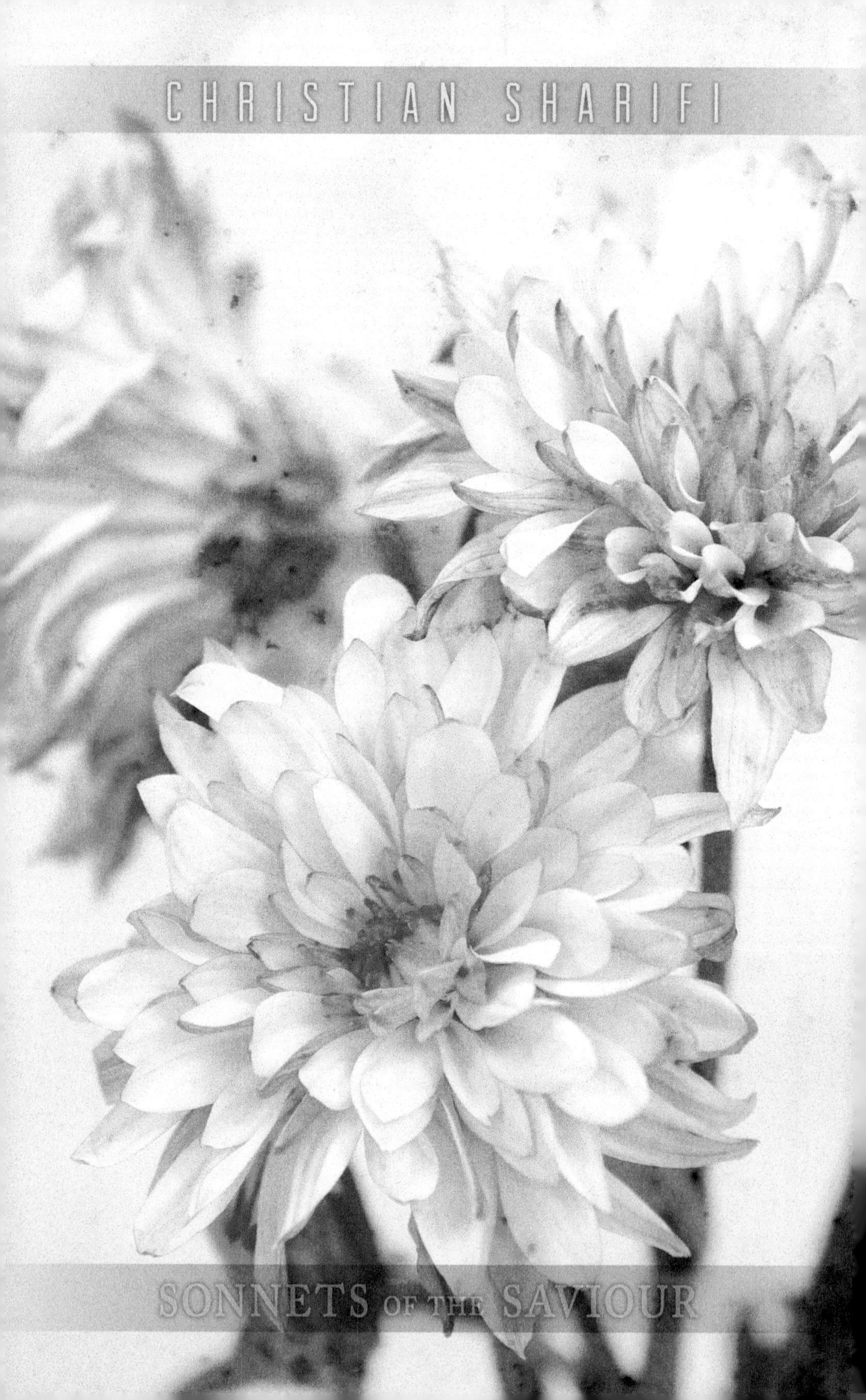
CHRISTIAN SHARIFI
SONNETS OF THE SAVIOUR

Poem 51

Praise the Lord in his sanctuary, bless our King in His courts

His presence protects me from the faculty of His fort

He came as a lamb, but is glorified as the lion

The enemies of the Most High, shall be cut down because of defiance.

His nobility is of grandeur abundance

Come to the King Most High, thou cease your reluctance

He was born of a manger, in the borough of Bethlehem

Soon after travailed in Egypt, to avert king Harod's plans

Howbeit that the son of Mary, could be the Son of God

Through him he has saved the sheep scattered abroad

The glory of our Lord shall endure forever

His blood shall cleanse the sins of whosoever

Let the heavens and the earth exalt our mighty majesty

No weapon formed against me shall prosper that is after me

His armor conserves my life and my families

Fostering my refuge of my futures ancestry

CHRISTIAN SHARIFI

SONNETS of the SAVIOUR

Poem 52

The land of the possessors belongs to the children of God

He makes a place of refuge and defense behind the heavenly walls

A vain heart shall pass on the redemption offered from the king

The wicked drown in the winter while the righteous blossom in the spring

The Holy laugh at death saying O'death, where is thy sting

To the promises of the Father do the righteous cling

The unveiling of his kingdom, is revealed to the lowly

To enter therein one must live a life pure, humble, and Holy

On the road to Jerusalem, there shall me many snakes and scorpions

The righteous suffer mockery and the wicked will always be scorning them

Sing unto the throne of grace because your salvation has drawn nigh

A believer of Christ is limitless, his future higher than the skies

Each soul has an ordained and designed path of life to walk

Jehovah sees all things, his eyes are as a hawk

The wicked are manhandled in a melee of brisk buffets

The righteous are shielded by a shield which cease not to always protect

Poem 53

An inferno of infirmities lay wait for the insensitive of heart

The peace of God fills the lowly but for sinners it departs

The impact of a heart felt prayer can move the foundation of mountains

Jesus is the living water and his glorious word is my fountain

In the tabernacle of justice the emperor shall reign with a rod

Yet his mercy endures forever as he forgives man for his flaws

Behold his ways were perfect, the son of the living GOD

His blood shall break down defeat like Jericho and its walls

On the day of judgement, man will have to give account

Shall your name be in the book of life, shall you wear your crown

There are merely two options, to rest in eternal rest

One shall gaze marvelous beauty, the other in eternal death

The pathway of the Godly, is the road to heavenly abodes

The roadway of the rebellious, shall lead an empty soul

The king shall wait at the gates to greet his trusty servant

He gained entrance because of God's laws was he observant

CHRISTIAN SHARIFI

SONNETS of the SAVIOUR

Poem 54

Hearken unto the commandments of the Mighty King

Rise early at dawn my son for it is time to sing

Proceed with an offering of dance to our gracious Overlord

He will punish your enemies' mercilessly with the blades of a sword

We were created to worship the beauty of his Holiness

Lack of praise is deemed the reason for man's loneliness

Thank him for the wonders he has bestowed upon your path

Praise him for his mercy and forgiveness of his wrath

Sow a seed and give to an orphan and it shall return in plenty

To give to the brethren shall never come back to you empty

In all my days I shall radiate his beauty with my speech

He is the treasure in my soul that makes my life complete

He destroys the destroyer and my enemies fall at defeat

Their foolish snares shall always be deemed bittersweet

My heart thirsts for greater peace in the midst of his presence

In his presence are presents for abundance is his essence

CHRISTIAN SHARIFI

SONNETS OF THE SAVIOUR

Poem 55

The temptations of the tempests are tribulations and travesty

Magnificent mandates make for morality from the mighty majesty

Erroneous excuses emulate from the empty and evil

Be benign and benevolent to the brethren and beseech them

Cordialness and compassion are the compass of the considerate

A softhearted soldier has a soft touch on the sailors that sail

Brutal barbarians are born bestial, bitter, and brutish

Ferocious fires of flames of fury are fierce and a fortress for the frank

Harsh and hateful hazards are hellish and horrible for the heartless

Soft sympathy sympathizes for the supportive and the sensitive

Wonderful wondrous wonders wait for the warm and warmhearted

Callous caretakers are careless and cold-hearted in common courtesy

Souls of the soulless are stiff and stony and their spirits are spiritless

Thick-skinned thieves are torpid and torturous in their thoughts

The tender touch of a teacher is thoughtful and true

A generation of gentleness grooms the gentiles for their good-nature

CHRISTIAN SHARIFI

SONNETS of the SAVIOUR

Poem 56

The angels in heaven sing songs for your glory

You are a God that worketh wonders, the beauty of his testimonies

The world marvels at your majestic manifold

The summer turns to winter, the heat turns to cold

In the vineyards shall I work, until my harvest bears fruit

In His word lies everlasting honesty in the depths of His truths

Mt. Zion rejoice, for the Lord has made your path brightened

Ask the Lord thy God to open your eyes of enlightenment

The Lord anger shall make the unjust stay frightened

He is my mighty avenger, the revenger to the titans

Keep those around you that have regard for his precepts

When judgement day comes, the sinners shall surely regret

Meditate on his word, so his laws can take hold of your soul

The Word of God is more precious than diamonds and gold

It shall direct your ways, and guide your life to wonder

It has the power to crush the enemies' plans comparable to thunder

CHRISTIAN SHARIFI

SONNETS OF THE SAVIOUR

Poem 57

Since the beginning of conception, thy word declared thy truth

His judgements remain just, they have prospered me since youth

I shall work all my days, sowing in thy field

Until the summer commences, and my harvest shall I yield

I keep the flock of my Father, as Moses did unto Jethro

The righteous desire righteousness, and their sins He shall let go

Two thousand years have passed, since my GOD walked the earth

I accepted him as my LORD, and on that day I was birthed

I seek his heart, his will, and his ways with all my essence

In life we learn from our mistakes, always adhere to lessons

The ungodly are filled with pressure and tormented by tensions

Strife, anger and malice encompass them in rivers of contention

Hearken diligently to the words of GOD and always pay close attention

For his words are like my wings leading me to great ascension

Principalities shall fall, and the wicked shall shed tears of agony

I shall in all my days sing songs of praise to my Mighty Majesty

CHRISTIAN SHARIFI

SONNETS of the SAVIOUR

Poem 58

Awe-inspiring awesomeness astounds Abba and is always amazing

Devine delight in delicious devotion and are deemed dynamite to demons

Respectful residents regard in respect and resilience for rural restrictions

Gracious and great Gabriel greets the GODLY at the gates of GOD

Calming and Courteous countenance of charming champions is celebrated

Endorse the elegance and emotions of the eleemosynary for eons

Benign benevolence of the big-hearted is bountiful and bounteous

Chivalrous chivalry copes the cures of the caring and compassionate

The congregation of the confident civilians cease not to console

My mother made me meek and mal-nourished in malice and mischievousness

The libertarian is liberal and lenient in laws and leniency

Rational and reasonable residents of Rome reap royal rewards

Self-sacrificing servants of the Savior are saved from sympathy

Endowed with esteem and excellence for El-Shaddai's elected elect

Auspicious amiable affections affects the amicable and always adoring

Confiding in a close confidant can close callouses and cure convulsions

CHRISTIAN SHARIFI

SONNETS of the SAVIOUR

Poem 59

Humanity has been engulfed in an unseen war from the unseen realm

Take heed, and protect yourself with the Word of GOD and its strength

The world shall pass, but his word shall retain glory for infinite eons

The power of sin and death has been eradicated and is now forgone

The insatiable amity towards Jehovah is eternally grafted on my heart

Through storms of trials and tribulation, our relationship shall never depart

Towards the end of my life, I offered a sacrifice of all my fine gold

And my redeemer rewarded me with virtues unto my soul

Day after day, and year after year, I harvest from the arms of the Almighty

In a deep pit of turmoil, was where El-Shaddai sought to find me

He rescued me from ravenous ravens, and protected me from the wolves

He abounded me in abundance, and built up all my walls

He calmed me in the tornado, and covered my soul by his wings

He is the Lord of all Lords, and shall always be the King of all Kings

In the middle of a melee, he raptured me from rioters

He exploited me from entanglement and captured me from the riotous

SONNETS OF THE SAVIOUR

Poem 60

Elohim sent his son, so that his children may live

Let us learn by his ways, and be mindful to give

The world is in his hands, the lands are in his gaze

Beyond eternal life, lies the detriment of flames

By freewill, we shall choose either life or death

Look up to the kingdom and climb their heavenly steps

His ways are colossal, his love lasts eminent

His mercy endureth forever, his forgiveness shines evident

His glory is a grand allure, his prestige is triumphant

His own people believed he was the one defiant

He sent King David to punish the giant

I glorify my God forever, my praise cease not in silence

Extol the splendor of our Savior, renowned his precious crown

The wedding supper of the lamb is near, so put on your wonderful gowns

The hour has come to travel home to our castle

Place the word in our hearts and let it rest upon the mantle

SONNETS of the SAVIOUR

Poem 61

My potential is potent for my poetry is pure, powerful and perfect

The descendants of deacons descended from diverse dews in the depths

Railers, rioters, and riotous revelers reap rotten redemptions

Shameless Sorcerers soliciting in sorcery soak in shame and sin

Correct and courteous chiefs of the church are conscientious and cordial

Immaculate and incorruptible indignities are intensely innocent

Mellow and merciful majesties are mild and moderate while magnanimous

The sons of sodomites and sworn satan's shall suffocate in a sea of sulfur

Abba is an all-knowing all-powerful absolute arch of armory

A careful Creator creates countries and continents correlating conciseness

Haste fully Honor the Holy-spirit who is Holy and honorable

Perilous and previse persecution pour profusely plumbing the pure

Gory and gross Groaning and gnashing germinate the guilty

God is great and glorious yet grand and grandeur in glorification

Patient people are purified and portray peace and are peace-loving

Silence of the still is smooth sails and a steady ship in the seas of Samaria

CHRISTIAN SHARIFI

SONNETS OF THE SAVIOUR

Poem 62

The word of GOD is a precious ointment proclaimed at the feet of Jesus

His laws and precepts I shall follow until the day I greet my leader

The brethren in Mt. Zion shall be strong and courageous like a fortress

While the demented deceitful shall be grotesque and morbid

In heaven the angels of GOD rejoice in his presence all their days

Embodied with the strength of an army each one attains in praise

The lion of the tribe of Judah has overcame the world and darkness

His heart is so heartily that he gave his own heart to the heartless

The downfall of the dying was that they do their own will

While a Doer of the precious word shall be planted on a Holy hill

In the middle of the night time, I shall awake to pray to God

I command fire from heaven to scatter my enemies abroad

His sanctuary is a place of safety, comfort, and tranquil peace

Face to face with demons, I kill when they come after me

Leave no room for satan, his snares are winey and cunning in plots

It's the anger of my Father, that plucks the devil with wroth

CHRISTIAN SHARIFI

SONNETS of the SAVIOUR

Poem 63

His exceeding greatness is greater than all the kingdoms on earth

The crown upon his head cannot be judged from the splendor of its worth

His white heavenly garment shines like a wise soul living by His Word

The wise men gave him royal gifts of frankincense and myrrh

I have forgave all my transgressors for He has forgiven me

My destiny is dependent solely on the amount of grace in me

I will never complain, speak guile, or lust for world and its evils

Instead I will rejoice in the author of my salvation and his elected people

He pulled me from the ploys of evil men and their conniving conspiracies

He granted me courage and boldness and dismantled any fear in me

The diabolical device maneuvers that lead to empty pits and graves

By the blood of Jesus Christ, shall humanity adhere to be saved

The atonement on the cross, despoiled my sins and wicked works

My enemies are deemed footstools, in the shadows they still lurk

No hell shall prevail against the Church of the living God

For Mt. Zion is a barricade and armory built on unbreakable walls

CHRISTIAN SHARIFI

SONNETS OF THE SAVIOUR

Poem 64

My master mandated Mt. Zion to magnify his majesties

Foresight and favor are formed from the Father to fix frustration

Havoc and hazardous hazards hover hugely over the horrible

Pure perfection parley pure perceptions as we praise in paradise

Sour and sorrowful sorcerers are saddened and sad-faced for being spiteful

Benign behavior brings blessing to the benevolent so bow before barons

Sodom is severed because of sorcerers and sodomites soliciting selfishly

Caring colleague can be companions and comrades to counsel a cohort

A prudent partner who is pure like poetry protects their persons

Mighty Moses was a man that was meeker than many men in the mainland

Woes, War and wrath wait in the wilderness for the wroth and wounded

Casual Christians can corrode as casualties for cause of contingency

Brazen and bold believers are a by-product of being big-hearted

Gentle gentiles are good-hearted and gracious to grieving guests

Unpleasant, Unfriendly, unkind, and ungenerous undergoes the ugly

Under the Unassuming, unresisting, and unpretentious is understanding

CHRISTIAN SHARIFI

SONNETS OF THE SAVIOUR

Poem 65

An unquenchable avidity burns inside to seek the King of the ages

Through temptations and sufferings he has begun in me new pages

My devotion and dedication is a manifestation of his divine grace

Always praying feverishly to enter paradise in that divine place

My passion and motive is formulated on his eternal sacrifice

Suphice to speak his word concisely from now until after life

No serpent, witch, or wizard shall ever have reign in my impulse

I shall throw daggers of fury and their grave shall be their final insult

Be blameless in walking in the ordinances and commandments of God

Be diligent in achieving your destiny and rising from the midst of fog

Accomplish all endeavors and arrange your goals based on His promise

The sprinkling of the blood of Jesus Christ shall clean a man's conscious

Anoint yourself in the oil of gladness and parlay in everlasting joy

For life is a journey of delight and our time on earth is to be enjoyed

Be conscious of blessing and endure to enter into a land of bliss

For by the mercies of GOD we are not destroyed and rescued from abyss

CHRISTIAN SHARIFI

SONNETS of the SAVIOUR

Poem 66

Sergeants and soldiers are sovereign and strive for salutations from the sultan

Often orchestrated and organized operations of the overlord are overt

Super superb statues of the Savior are super-eminent and stupendous

Wisdom of the warm and worthy are welcomed by wonderful warriors

Total triumph tails tycoons from Tennessee to
Tallahassee to tower over the torpid

Undependable, unsound and uncertainty under-
lay the underclass of the underworld

Foresight and favor forever forms a farmer for functioning in fineness

A master's morality merits meek morals in a man of meekness and mildness

Genes of a genius are genuine guidelines of God gathering in a gentleman

Follow figures who figurehead the Father and his fatherly fondness

Taste the tender tenderness of a tolerable and timid trader and toiler

White-collar workers work wonderfully with wonder in a wonderland

Totalistic totalitarianism trends over torpid and terrible tribes or terror

Correlate collective conscious of consciousness to collaborate care and charity

Devine divinity is demonstrated and dictated from deacons of devotion

Dislike deities of a demigod or demon for their dementedness and debauchery

CHRISTIAN SHARIFI

SONNETS OF THE SAVIOUR

Poem 67

A furnace of sweltering torridness is the destination of the diabolical

A fiery fever formulates and engulfs the ungodly in a sea of trouble

The flare upon the tempter is a holocaust of hazardous coals burning

Furious infernos are an ocean of flames to the unrighteous railer

Explosions of tinder encompass evil witches and their vial covens

The cross fire of the Holy Ghost shall snipe the sorcerers encampments

A shelling of hail storms of anger shall pour upon the rivals of Jehovah

The saboteur organizes a sabotage with a villainous countenance

His devices are dormant as my GOD deploys his angels of war

The strategy of the spiteful is to derail the masters of meekness

Rancorous rascals run about ruining the rewards of the righteous

Poisonous words depart from the mouths of repulsive agents

A blazing brimstone of agony await foul servants of the devil

Villainous villains are often offensive and offend the pellucid

The luminous attain lumination with translucent transparency

Pleasant servanthood is a mandate for the monarchs of nobility

CHRISTIAN SHARIFI

SONNETS OF THE SAVIOUR

Poem 68

A vile person only honors his selfish internal desires

A person of honor honors our GOD to exalt Him higher

A greedy man shall be bewildered with the spirit of grief

A patient person of purity shall show mercy unto a thief

A foul fellow beguiles deceit from the day of the womb

A benign bloke shall flourish as a rose about to bloom

A corrupt citizen is walking straight to a dungeon of doom

A repented soul has staggered not to rise out the tomb

The murderous mason is a destroyer of the salutary of the saint

The beauty of the beautiful shall make the wicked faint

Egotistical egos are thrown with no mercy into a black hole

The charitable in their heart of hearts have no desire to act cold

The obscene are always an obstacle for the righteous to hurdle

By no means shall the son of a child of GOD ever desire to hurt you

A spiteful spirit has no grounds to forgive a person's wrong doing

A humane human dines with kings in the council of the ruling

CHRISTIAN SHARIFI

SONNETS of the SAVIOUR

Poem 69

The diabolical are drowned In a pool of sinful blood

Sorcerers and witches shall remain obsessed in dabbing with their drugs

Fornicators are butchered when the almighty makes avenge

Mercy flows through his veins but a time shall come for revenge

Extortioners are excited out of Eden for indecent behavior

Companions of callus men shall ooze the same defiled savor

Taphobia is a symptom of the enemies of our Creator

The air of the atrocious shall be cut off by the great deflator

The burial of the brazen brutes shall be buried alive

The presence of God for his children carries them high

The anointing of the Holy Ghost sustains power of boldness

The offspring of lucifer's children are frozen in coldness

Surround yourself with men like Joshua and Caleb

Able to conquer the conquerors with power to slay them

The spirit of Moses was meekest upon all of the lands

Thus The Lord thy God revealed unto him his glorious plans

CHRISTIAN SHARIFI

SONNETS OF THE SAVIOUR

Poem 70

Quit quarrelling with the quarrelsome and their quests

Instead ignite your inner inhibitions internally infused

Behold beneath the bosom of the bodacious barons beacon

The totality of the triumph of the triumphant towers in the tabernacle

Celebrate the charm and charisma of Christ the Creator

The doorway to dormant drive is deemed through depravity

The foulness of fornicators is foul to the Father's face

A Father to the fatherless facilitates fortune for the fair

Riotous rioters riot and rape the righteousness of the righteous

His highness has half their Hines in a harvest of homicide

Everlasting enticement entices the evil with envious envy

The painful persist in pain and perdition permanently

The hearty have a half heart and are hazards to the hole some

Paying the price of promiscuousness pails to people permeating prosperity

Living lay waste in laviciousness is a loss for the lonely

Regeneration radiates rascals and reprobates into redeemed

CHRISTIAN SHARIFI

SONNETS OF THE SAVIOUR

Poem 71

The sluggard struggles for his hands are idle in the garden

The ant is a prime example of diligence for in due time he shall harvest

A lazy worker gossips with his mouth rather than labouring with strength

The owner of the farm sows seeds while the sluggard sits on the bench

In the middle of a blizzard the task master is mastering his tasks

The laggard is lackadaisical like Lazarus drinking from his flask

An attentive associate attends to attention to finish His assignment

A deranged labourer is a thief in his heart and lives in defilement

Prudent manners perfect the perilous of a grinding career

The languorous are lifeless and are blind for they cannot see clear

The constant consistency of a caretaker takes care of his cares

The dallying and the drowsy are dull and desperately need prayers

Assertive activity brings assiduity to a farmer's son

For he labours when there is no light and ends when there is no sun

A gentlemen that is weak in strength is a fool in the eye of God

A lethargic slack shall lose His income and equity to a hound of dogs

CHRISTIAN SHARIFI

SONNETS of the SAVIOUR

Poem 72

Praises echo from the tower of cathedrals across the globe

The high priest is the shepherd and watches over their souls

Through rebukes and chastisements does the child grow and mature

Judgement falls on the price of sin and there is only one cure

Finding true fulfillment is only in the hands of our GOD

Seeking real gratification comes from the one high above

The Sabbath is a day to praise and worship the Creator of all

The evil seeds that roam in the earth have already began to fall

The rights of the righteous is to prosper in all the land

Vindictive villains shall crumble in the Savior's mighty hands

The Lord seeks vengeance on the vengeful and to break their bands

The Lord bestows mercy on the gracious and restores their plans

The council of the counsellors shall lead you out of the wilderness

The wisdom of the wise shall serve you out of baroness

Vagabonds and hooligans walk the streets with no destination at night

Those planted in the house of the Lord shall shine a radiance of light

CHRISTIAN SHARIFI

SONNETS of the SAVIOUR

Poem 73

I shall dwell in the sanctuary of my Savior for all my days

I will rejoice in his good works and sing in songs of praise

I adore his tender heart and I desire to sit at his right hand

The time span of his mercy is infinite like the grains of sand

I spend my life seeking the one who also seeks me

He destroyed my yokes now as a bird I finally feel free

In my weakness I am strong by his reigning power

Jehovah created the stars and the comets that shower

The fowls of the air and the beasts of the land are in his hands

The throne room of God is enticing and draped in grand

His angels sing day and night lifting the name of the Most high

While sinners' hearts are frozen and their face is a cold sigh

Jesus was the Lamb of God, but is now glorified as the lion

He butchered the plans of satan as David annihilated Goliath

The spirit of Elijah shall dismantle the plans of the tempter

By the grace of God, the heavenly gates I shall enter

CHRISTIAN SHARIFI

SONNETS OF THE SAVIOUR

Poem 74

Closed curtains of catastrophes castrate cold criminals

While worthy and warm wonders wait for the wonderful

Future fate of the foul is forgone in a frenzy of funerals

Benevolent and benign brothers are beneficiary to beautiful blessings

Indecent idiots imply immorality in incense and indecent inceptions

The totality of the tolerable is a tower of thoughtfulness and tender hearts

Cold blooded and callous cleave to calamity and cessations

Emotions of enjoyment envelop Elohim's elected elect

Vicious villains are villainous and vile vermin with vindictive vindication

Huge hearts of humane humanitarians harvest hefty harvests

Extreme Evil exists in the exorcists of the execrable enchanters

Appreciation and adulation await the armor of amorousness angels

Intense injury and irritation is infinite in the intentions of the injurious

Courteous and consideration care caresses for commendable children

Anguish and anger are always the attitude of the antagonized

Respectful residents of royalty relish and regard rules and restrictions

CHRISTIAN SHARIFI

SONNETS of the SAVIOUR

Poem 75

He that wondereth away from the path of understanding shall die

A man that forsakes the laws of the LORD is a fool in his eyes

The pride of life and the lusts of the flesh are from the enemy

The soldiers of God are created from a powerful pedigree

Blood thirsty brutes are brutal in their conscious and thought life

Alone I can do nothing, but with his spirit I walk in Gods might

My potential is potent for my poetry is pure and charming in nature

His words are an open river to my soul and come from the mouth of the Savior

The charisma of my Father is charming beyond imagination

At the gates of heaven I shall kneel and bow in salutations

Blessings rain on the head of the sanctified and the Holy children

Before he formed me, he knew me, and has now sent me on my mission

Why do the enemies of God seek vain snares for they are senseless

They shall never take the royal crown of my Father or touch his scepter

Jesus Christ created the whole world in a span of six days

He will judge the unjust and mock them for their sick ways

CHRISTIAN SHARIFI

SONNETS of the SAVIOUR

Poem 76

A mission ordained by the Father to rescue humanity from their wickedness

By His own virtue the Lord came from heaven to earth thus was heaven-sent

By His own mercy, he sacrificed His life bearing the stripes for our iniquities

The sins of all mankind rest on His shoulders from now until infinite

Yet freewill is a dangerous weapon, with it we choose either life or death

Accepting Christ will dictate where man spends eternity after final breath

Hellfire awaits the prideful, while streets of gold cover the gracious

Solomon spoke how life is meaningless like never ending mazes

Every man will be sent to the judgement seat of the judge and jury

While the humble shall be forgiven, and the sinner entrenched in His fury

Demons wait in Hades for the souls who have failed in reaching salvation

Mansions wait in the kingdom of GOD for
souls who have waited with patience

Man could die at any minute, hour, or second, yet he lives his life amiss

Lazarus sojourned in Abraham's bosom while the rich man fell to the abyss

The thief on the cross, repented in the very last seconds of his earthly life

The other thief rejected the Savior, thus rejecting pearly gates in the afterlife

CHRISTIAN SHARIFI

SONNETS of the SAVIOUR

Poem 77

Softhearted souls seek the safety and security of El Shaddai

Rancorous Reprobate rioters are revolting and repugnant

Perfection permeates the prosperity of pellucid patriarchs

Insane immediate Incest instills idiotic iniquitous imbeciles

Fathom and fires frustrate the farmers of a flagitious foul felon

Why worry when the woes of the wrongful wicked will wipe them

Stay silent and sojourn to salutary shores and stay serene and storm less

Embark on Elohim's elegance and esteem His eternally encompassing enigma

Journey to Jehova's judicature to joy in jubilance and juristic junctures

Harmonizing healing hands of Hosanna has har-
vested havoc to horrendous heathens

Poisonous portals portraying peoples past puts the pure in perilousness

A Father facilitates fortune and finances to the fostering of the fatherless

Love and laugh loudly at the loveliness of the Lord of Lords leniency

Praise the perfectness of perfection that permeates profoundly from pure people

Under unrighteous and untamed understand-
ing does the uncivilized underappreciate

CHRISTIAN SHARIFI

SONNETS of the SAVIOUR

Poem 78

The oracles of GOD are ordained to lead man into delightful obedience

A Christian that obtains power has rules which are never lenient

The sons of man have put-fourth righteousness in their heart of hearts

The son of perdition shall not escape eternal hellfire in the darkest darks

The sweet smell of savor permeates the sky as I give offerings to my Lord

Failing to yield to His laws is a price no man can afford

My trust and my shield is proclaimed in the unseen hierarchy

My salutations belong to the mighty one of wrath who always shall guard me

The number of souls headed to destruction is broad beyond belief

The multitude of the righteous are the souls that washed their feet

For the feet of a man represent the entire being of that creation

The Lord thy GOD shall have all my enemies dead at derision

On the frontline of a war amongst the heavenliness and their counterparts

The Lord displaced satan from heaven and placed him in the outer parts

Why do the kings of destitute deviate from the precepts of my heavenly Father

Lawlessness and prodigality punish the perilous ones of no honor

CHRISTIAN SHARIFI

SONNETS of the SAVIOUR

Poem 79

Adore the virtue of our Lord as you praise his handwork

Praise him for his power and perfection in creating the earth

His children rejoice in the majesty of his mercy

His enemies tumble and fall and their judgement comes quickly

The entanglements of enchanters is everlasting fire

The fate of the un- fathomable is tormenting and shall be dyer

The precious sons of the Father are refined in their soul with a flame

The orphans of the Devil are rebels without a name

The days of the deceptive are short and sharp like a splinter

The life of the lowly appears them before heavens gates as they enter

A sinner ploys and preys on the in Innocent with cowardice schemes of injustice

The righteous command fire from heaven as Elijah shall rain down judgements

The front lines of this war are not for the faint of heart

The warriors of Jehovah have been trained to kill demons from the dark

With every new dispensation comes new mandates and authorities

The righteous shall never bow at unruly men and their conformities

CHRISTIAN SHARIFI

SONNETS of the SAVIOUR

Poem 80

Rejoice for today is the day that The Lord has made

In His tabernacle of truth shall my soul forever praise

I travail in my prayers until my destiny unfolds

My being yearns for His presence, my heart yearns for His soul

Separation with my Father is torture to my bones

The day shall come to pass when I enter my heavenly home

The cedars of Lebanon grow as I do In His precepts

A sinner shall buckle under the envelope of regret

The lion is the greatest amongst the beasts in its kingdom

A man that lacks destiny is a man that lacks vision

Inquire from The Lord from lessons you understand not

A thief escapes for a moment but In the end he shall be caught

The cost of prodigality is the same cost as eternal hellfire

The dreams of my destiny are the ones I must aim higher

The ending of a bastard is the same as the devils climax

Born again in the spirit means my God remembers not my past

CHRISTIAN SHARIFI

Poem 81

Abundant abundance dwells in the chamber of the righteous ones

Poverty of pestilence inhibited the land of the wicked sons

Emasculate joy covers the radiance of the sanctified descendants

By his mercy alone, is man found not guilty as the defendant

Prosperity prospers the children that convey honor

Profoundness personifies the beauty of my Father

Impart into me O LORD, the spirit of thy faith

Grant me the glory my GOD, of the abundance of thy grace

Allow me awe sight, as I enter the house of Elohim

Heal my afflictions, from the enemies' widely schemes

Mt Zion is my nest, the sanctuary of my refuge

Established as a house of prayer and wisdom of thy truths

A thousand days cannot compare to one in your cathedral

Even when the flesh ceases existence, I shall never cease to leave you

Eternal breath lay waiting as I walk thy eternal steps

Infinite blessings pour thunder for I am eternal blessed

CPSIA information can be obtained
at www.ICGtesting.com
Printed in the USA
LVOW05*1052090316

478321LV00003B/3/P

To My Dear Sister,
Please enjoy This book

from brother